Botanical Colour at your Fingertips

REBECCA DESNOS

Botanical Colour at your Fingertips
Published in 2016 by Rebecca Desnos
www.rebeccadesnos.com

Second Edition

The information in this book is true
and complete to the best of the author's
knowledge. All recommendations are made
without guarantee. The author has made
every effort to ensure that all instructions
given in this book are accurate and safe, but
cannot accept liability, whether direct or
consquential, however arising.

ISBN: 978-0-9955566-2-1

All photography by Rebecca Desnos,
except the portrait on page 106 by
Kasia Fiszer.

Hand lettering by Katrina Sophia.

contents

	my story	7
section 1	introduction	9
section 2	my approach to plant dyeing	21
section 3	gathering plants	31
section 4	equipment & safety	45
section 5	washing & mordanting fibres	49
section 6	making a dye bath	57
section 7	dyeing fabric & yarn	71
section 8	iron water	81
section 9	colour fastness	91
	what next?	99
	glossary	100
	UK/US vocabulary differences	102
	bibliography	105
	about the author	106

my story

I began plant dyeing several years ago by experimenting with powdered dye extracts and chemical assistants (known as mordants) to fix dyes to fabric. It didn't take me long to become captivated by the rainbow of colours that nature has to offer. As I became more immersed in dyeing, I began to search for a deeper connection with the plants I was dyeing with, so I chose to use fresh plants rather than extracts. There is so much colour potential around us, in the form of kitchen food waste, cultivated plants in the garden and local wild plants, that I don't feel compelled to purchase powdered dye anymore. The process of gathering plants and extracting the dye is so fulfilling. We literally have colour right at our fingertips waiting to be unlocked, which was my inspiration for the title!

Whilst searching for a deeper connection with nature, I started to question the mordants I was using to fix the colours. I felt like I was infusing my natural fabrics with synthetic and arguably toxic chemicals, which seemed incongruous to my own ethics of leading a natural and organic lifestyle. I soon learnt that it was possible to use soya milk to bind plant dyes to fibres. Since then, I've never gone back to my old methods as soya milk works exceptionally well. Along the way, I learnt that many dye plants contain tannins that naturally bond to fibres. Plants contain everything within them to produce longlasting colours; additional chemicals simply are not necessary. Plants are truly magic!

Within these pages you will find everything you need to start your journey with plant dyeing. Even if you have dyed with plants before, I hope that you will still find something useful here.

introduction

*The difference between cellulose and protein fibres,
substantive and adjective dyes,
and why mordants are an important part of the dyeing process.*

My methods

The beauty of plant dyeing is that there are so many methods for producing colour on fabric and yarn. There isn't just one 'right way'. In this book I share my own natural processes for creating long-lasting colours.

Most plants produce some kind of colour but it is certainly true that some plants make better dyes than others. This book will show you how to make long-lasting colours with some 'tried and tested' plants, but it is also exciting to experiment with other plants where the results may be unknown.

I like to use a combination of these two approaches; using my favourite plants to produce reliable dyes (especially when I intend to sell dyed textiles) whilst continuing to explore different plants. Each time I experiment with a new plant I inevitably learn something, so all experiments are worthwhile.

Dyeing with whole dyestuffs

In this book we will dye with 'whole dyestuffs' which means that we will use whole plants, either fresh or dried. I'll show you how to exploit the colour potential of plants that grow in the wild, garden herbs, kitchen waste, as well as fruit and vegetables that you can buy from the supermarket. There is colour potential all around us waiting to be used!

Greys from lavender & tans from thyme

Substantive dyes

Avocado stones &
pomegranate skins

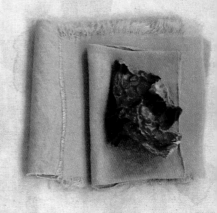

Adjective dyes

Mahonia berries &
dandelion flowers

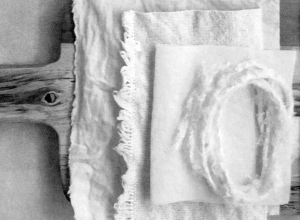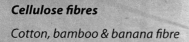

Cellulose fibres

Cotton, bamboo & banana fibre

Protein fibres

Soybean (also wool & silk)

Different types of plant dye

There are different types of plant dye and they bond to the fibres in different ways.

1. **Substantive dyes,** such as pomegranate skins, avocado stones and tea contain substances called tannins which act as a natural mordant and help bond the dyes to the fibres.

   - A sub-category of substantive dyes is **vat dyes**, which include indigo and woad. These require a reduction agent to remove the oxygen to make the dye soluble in water in order for the dye to bond with fibres, and are beyond the scope of this book.

2. **Adjective dyes,** such as dyes from flowers and berries, need help from another substance, known as a mordant, to bind the dye to fibres. Without a mordant the colours will not last long.

Different types of fibre

Fibres are either of protein or cellulose origin.

1. **Cellulose fibres,** such as cotton, linen, hemp and bamboo viscose, come from plants and need assistance from a mordant to bind with plant dyes. Without mordanting, the colours are usually pale and wash out quickly.

2. **Protein fibres,** such as wool, silk and soybean, have a natural affinity with plant dyes and readily absorb colour. In general terms it can be said that they do not require mordanting. Protein fibres are usually from animals, although soybean fibre is an exception. I choose to work with vegan fibres so the only protein fibres in this book are from soybeans.

Mordants

A mordant is a substance that assists with the bond between the dye and fibre. Cellulose fibres, like cotton, need some assistance in order to be successfully dyed with plants.

The main mordant used in this book is soybean protein in the form of soya milk. Cellulose fibres soaked in soya milk absorb some of the soy protein, which changes the properties of the fibres so they become similar to protein fibres. Like naturally occuring protein fibres, cellulose fibres that have been pretreated with soya milk then have a natural affinity to plant dyes. These mordanted fibres will absorb more dye which results in darker colours which are also more colour fast. The soybean protein increases the bond between the fibre and the dye.

Many dyes also contain natural mordants in the form of tannins. By using a combination of the soya milk mordanting method and tannin rich dyes, we can achieve long-lasting and most importantly 100% natural colours.

Why I don't use alum

Alum is a popular mordant and is widely known as the 'least toxic' metallic salt mordant. However, it must be noted that aluminium is in fact a toxin to the human body. When handling alum, a dust mask is advisable and care should be taken to not inhale the acidic vapours from the dye pot. Without a doubt there are potential health risks from working with alum. I find the soya milk mordanting method produces better results in terms of colour fastness, so I feel no need to use alum again.

Some of the natural mordants in this book

Bamboo
no soya

Bamboo
+ soya

Organic
cotton + soya

Soybean
jersey

Bamboo + soya

Bamboo
no soya

Organic cotton
no soya

Soybean
jersey

Lavender Leaves

Red Onion Skins

The fibres and dyes in this book

This book focuses on dyeing plant fibres with substantive and adjective dyes, whilst using natural mordanting methods.

Throughout this book I have chosen to work with only plant fibres, and this is because I am vegan. I use cellulose fibres such as cotton, linen, banana fibre and bamboo, as well as soybean fibre which is a protein fibre. It is true in general that animal protein fibres dye much more easily than cellulose fibres, but pretreating cellulose fibres with soya milk effectively transforms them into protein fibres.

As a vegan natural dyer, I was particularly excited to come across soybean fibre a few years ago. This plant protein fibre dyes exceptionally well and soya fabric is silky soft.

My personal ethics are instilled in my textile practice, but of course you may choose to dye animal protein fibres. You will no doubt discover that you can easily achieve dark colours and possibly need less dyestuff than I use when dyeing cellulose fibres.

Even though many substantive dyes contain their own natural mordants in the form of tannins, fibres still benefit from being mordanted with soya milk to increase the uptake of dye. Mordanting helps produce deeper colours, especially on cellulose fibres, and can also widen the range of colours that a plant produces. A spectacular example is red onion skin dye that produces green on unmordanted cellulose fibres, but dark brown on the same fibres pretreated with soya milk.

Palette of colours

The photo opposite shows the range of colours produced from some of the dye plants in this book. These exact colours aren't guaranteed; the outcome depends on the growing conditions of the plants and any dissolved minerals in your tap water.

Substantive dyes which contain tannins produce particularly colour fast dyes and are marked with an asterix (*) below.

1. * avocado stones
2. * avocado skins
3. hibiscus flowers (acid modified)
4. mahonia berries (acid modified)
5. mahonia berries
6. * nettles
7. hibiscus flowers
8. carrot tops
9. daffodils
10. * pomegranate skins
11. * red onion skins (no mordant)
12. * alder cones
13. * black tea
14. * red onion skins (mordant)
15. mint
16. bay leaves
17. * eucalyptus leaves
18. * alder catkins
19. * rooibos tea
20. * rosemary
21. * lavender leaves

What about blue and green?

We will not work with vat dyes such as indigo and woad to produce blues, as these dyes require specialist techniques. Dyeing with vat dyes is easily achievable at home and you may choose to overdye yellows to make colour fast greens. Alternatively you can make green from onion skins and a less colour fast green from carrot tops. A range of grey-blues can be made from berries (which contain anthocyanin pigments); pinks from berries turn blue under tap water due to the pH change, then return to pink in acidic conditions.

my approach to plant dyeing

*The four crucial principles that I follow when dyeing cellulose fibres
to ensure that colours are rich and, most importantly, long-lasting.*

1. Pretreating fibres in soya milk

Protein fibres such as wool and silk have a natural affinity with plant dyes. When cellulose fibres are soaked in soya milk, the soybean protein coats the fibres and the fibres become more like protein fibres. Cotton that has been pretreated in soya milk adopts some of the qualities of protein fibres and absorbs much more dye than untreated cotton.

Soybeans contain up to 40% protein and there is a component within soya protein that acts as a binding agent. Soya has the ability to bind natural dyes to cloth extremely well, especially if the soya milk mordanted fabric or yarn is left for some time before dyeing to allow the protein to fully bond to the fibres.

Soya mordanting is a centuries old method that has been used in many cultures across the world. Perhaps the most well known example is the Japanese stencil resist dyeing technique of Katazone, where fabric is sized with soya milk, then painted with pigments that have been mixed with soya milk.

Soybean protein is such a good binding agent that even silk can benefit from soya milk treatment. Other sources of protein have potential for binding dyes, ranging from plant proteins from acorns and rice, to animal milks and egg whites.

Lavender leaves

Red onion skin

Thyme

Avocado stones

Pomegranate skin

Hibiscus flowers

Within each pile of cotton swatches
the one on the left was pretreated in soya milk & the one on the right was untreated

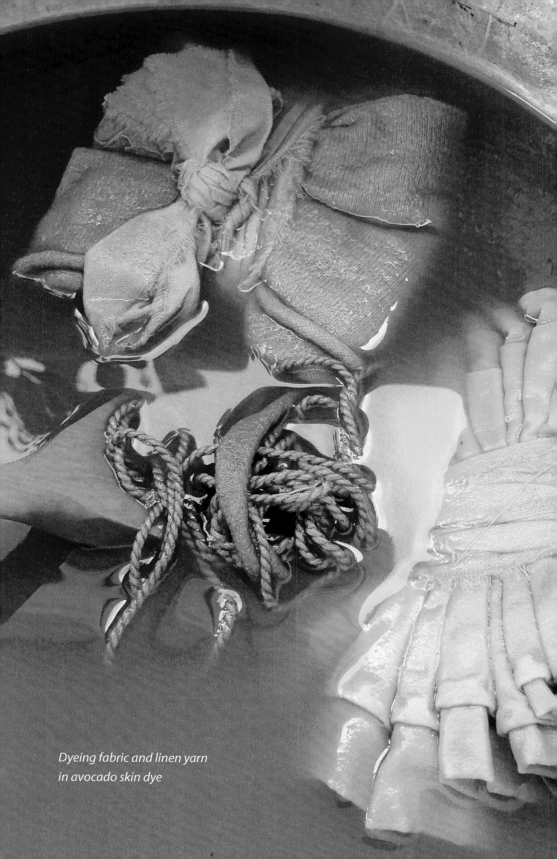

*Dyeing fabric and linen yarn
in avocado skin dye*

2. Using a pot as a mordant

If we decide to avoid using metallic salt mordants such as alum, that doesn't mean that we cannot benefit from the 'mordanting potential' of metals. By simply using an aluminium pot, we will get a similar benefit as mordanting with alum but without handling fine powders. Since we need to use a dye pot of some kind, we may as well choose one with a metal that is useful to us, rather than using stainless steel which is non reactive.

The longer the dye is left in the pot, the more of an influence there is from the metal. I do all my dyeing in aluminium pots and dye slowly for long periods of time to get the maximum benefit from the metal in the pot.

Dye particles are attracted to the side of the pot as dye reacts with the metal. The build up of dye can be washed off with a scouring sponge at the end of each dyeing session. It is this reactive nature of aluminium that we take advantage of when using a pot as a mordant.

I have found some plant dyes to be 'cleansing' and effectively clean off the build up of dye inside the pot. After dyeing with a dark tannin rich dye, I often boil some dried hibiscus flowers in water to clean my pot.

Aluminium pots are known to help brighten colours and in my experience the metal can often bring out entirely different shades. A dye may begin as a pale yellow and slowly transform into a different colour over the course of a day or two. I've seen this with lavender and rosemary dye, as well as many other leaves and flowers.

Iron and copper pots can also be used for different effects; iron darkens colours and copper enhances yellows. It's fascinating to dye with different kinds of pots to see the wide range of colours that a single plant can yield.

3. Using dyes rich in tannins

Tannins are naturally occurring compounds found in seeds, leaves, bark and fruit. Tannins are usually yellow or brown in colour and taste bitter. They are found in grapes and play a role in wine making and are responsible for making some types of wine taste bitter. Tannins are also in tea, in varying amounts, explaining why some types of tea taste more bitter than others.

Tannins are extremely useful in dyeing as they have the ability to help fix dyes to fibres by acting as mordants. Some tannins are clear coloured (such as those found in oak galls) and light coloured (such as those in pomegranate skins) and can be applied to fibres to improve the colour fastness of other dyes applied afterwards.

Cellulose fabrics can actually be dyed with tannin rich dyes without soya milk mordanting, but the additional step of soya milk treatment undoubtedly produces much deeper shades.

Dyes which contain high levels of tannins certainly produce reliable and long-lasting colours which are essential qualities when selling dyed textiles, but it is still worth experimenting with other potentially less colour fast dyes. I try not to become so preoccupied with colour fastness that I am scared to experiment with plants that do not contain tannins in case the colour fades. It is fun to try new plants, especially when dyeing fabric for personal use. The topic of colour fastness is explored further in Section 9.

Colours clockwise from top left:

avocado stones (second dye bath), pomegranate skins,

avocado stones (first dye bath), nettles

*Experimenting with dye
made from rosemary*

4. Time

The longest lasting colours come when plenty of time has been spent on the entire process. It is worth emphasising that 'time' does not equal 'effort'; many of the processes in this book take a long time, but require little effort. The processes simply need to be set up and monitored and left for a period of time for full effect.

I usually have several projects on the go at once at various stages and do a little bit of everything every day. At any one time, I may have fabric or yarn soaking in a bucket of soya milk, a pot of dye on the stove either heating or soaking, a pile of fabric in the cupboard that has been treated with soya milk and other fabric waiting to be rinsed and washed after dyeing.

It is worth keeping a stash of soya milk treated fabric or yarn ready for impromptu dyeing sessions. After mordanting, the fibres are best left for a minimum of a week before dyeing, ideally longer. The soya protein becomes part of the fibres and time is needed for this process to take place.

Preparing a dye bath also takes time and this can rarely be done in a single day. Colours take time to fully extract from plants and then the fibres take time to absorb and bond with the dye. Generally, the longer you spend on each step, the better the results will be.

Plant dyeing is a slow process and it is this very aspect that I love most; it is an antidote to a hectic life. The process is just as enjoyable as the final result and I savour every moment. In my opinion, the colours from nature are far superior to synthetic colours, so the time is well worth spending.

SECTION 3
gathering plants

A guide to choosing and storing dye plants,
and pages of colour swatches showing potential dye colours from plants.

Choosing dye plants

Almost every plant has some kind of colour potential, although some plants produce stronger and more colour fast dyes than others.

Some plants that contain dye pigments can be identified by their Latin names which often include 'tinctoria', such as *Rubia tinctoria* (madder) and *Anthemis tinctoria* (chamomile). However, many of the plants in this book are not traditional dye plants, so this section offers some suggestions for choosing plants that give promising results in the dye pot.

Storing plants

Plants may produce different colours depending on whether they are used fresh or dry. I like to store dried plants in cardboard boxes to let the air flow and prevent mildew forming. You may choose to freeze some dyestuffs, although I try to avoid freezing too much due to the cost of running the freezer but I sometimes freeze flowers.

If you would like to make dye from fresh plants but don't have any mordanted fabric or yarn, you can make concentrated dye (by using very little water) and store it in an airtight jar in the fridge until you are ready to use it. Then pour it into the dye pot and add as much extra water as you need.

Bay leaves

Lavender

Eucalyptus leaves

Plants with scent

My favourite tip for identifying promising dye plants comes from India Flint, who recommends looking out for plants with a scent. This indicates the presence of aromatic oils and acids which suggests that the plant has dye potential.

Eucalyptus is a perfect example of this; the leaves contain eucalyptus oil and they certainly produce spectacular colours in the dye pot. Other examples include bay leaves and lavender, but of course many other herbs.

To see if you have extracted as much dye as possible into the water, simply take a leaf out of the dye pot and smell it. If it no longer has any scent then you have probably extracted all of the available colour. But if it still smells, try heating it in fresh water to extract even more colour, then combine the two lots of dye.

Colour variation

There are so many factors involved in plant dyeing that there is no guarantee that you will get the same colour twice. This can be frustrating when trying to replicate colours but it is also one of the most exciting aspects of plant dyeing. There is always an element of surprise!

The location where the plant is grown can affect the colour outcome (soil, water and weather conditions) as well as the time of year and how mature the plant is. Even when dyeing with your favourite plants, there is always an element of uncertainty. I have noticed that Hass avocado skins produce slightly different shades throughout the year. Nettles produce any colour from light grey to olive green. Plant dyeing on holiday can give surprising results due to the different tap water and growing conditions of plants.

Plants in the wild

Naturally, our place in the world will determine exactly which plants grow locally. You may find that you question the dyeing potential of almost every plant you come across which adds a stimulating new element to local walks. Through research and exploration you will become an expert on your local dye plants and your colours will be unique to your region.

It is important to find out the name of any plant you may wish to use and to check that it is not poisonous. Some plants may be toxic when ingested, which is especially dangerous when children collect plants. With other plants, the fumes from the dye pot may be harmful to inhale, most notably in the case of rhubarb leaves which contain oxalic acid.

Remember that plants are part of a delicate ecosystem and we must respect this when collecting from the wild. Here are some things that I like to keep in mind when foraging for plants:

- Collect wind fallen plant matter first and then weeds that grow invasively.

- As a guide, do not pick more than 10% of flowers, berries or leaves.

- Remember that small creatures depend on flowers and berries for their sustenance.

- It's important to leave enough flowers so they can self-seed the following season.

- Only remove bark from fallen branches (e.g. after a storm). Peeling off too much bark from the trunk can actually kill trees.

Alder catkins

Dandelions

Alder cones

Daffodils

Nettles

Mint

Rosemary

Thyme

Plants from the garden

In your garden you may already have fruit trees such as apple, cherry or pear from which you can collect leaves and bark. If you live in a warmer part of the world you may have more exotic trees growing, such as pomegranate or avocado.

Perhaps you already grow herbs which would make an excellent starting point for dyeing. You could keep a few pots on a windowsill or balcony, for smaller experiments. If you are lucky enough to have a larger space, you may decide to plant your own dye garden with traditional dye plants.

Don't despair if you don't have your own garden. Once your friends and family learn that you dye with plants, you may well find that they are more than happy to offer you anything you like from their garden. People are usually so fascinated by plant dyeing and only too keen to offer plants. It's also worth talking to neighbours and asking if you can have any prunings from their gardens.

The dyes from mint and thyme (opposite) are subtle but beautiful. Rosemary produces much more intense colours and I have found that different varieties of rosemary produce different shades of brown and grey. One variety of rosemary even makes purple dye in an aluminium pot which was an exciting discovery for me (photo on page 28). It is these surprising results that make plant dyeing so thrilling!

Dyes from the kitchen

The food you enjoy eating may determine what you dye with or it may be the other way round. I often find myself shopping for food with dye potential on my mind!

You might collect onion skins, avocado stones and skins and pomegranate skins, all of which make beautiful dyes. Tea, herbs and carrot tops also produce lovely colours, as do many other fruits and vegetables.

Bear in mind that beetroot may at first seem like a perfect dye, but the betalain pigments found in beetroot are fugitive, which means that the colour will fade away, perhaps months or years later, even without exposure to light. Sometimes plants that give up their colour so quickly do not make the best dyes.

It is worth experimenting with berries; they contain tannins in varying amounts and can produce lovely grey-blues when rinsed under tap water, which return to pink when rinsed in vinegar water.

Carrot tops

Rooibos tea

Dried hibiscus
flower tea

Red onion skins

Black tea

Pomegranate skins

Avocado stones and skins

Tannin rich dyes from the kitchen

Some of my favourite tannin rich and very reliable dyes come from kitchen food waste. Tea is a perfect example of this; you can simply save used tea bags and add them into a dye pot of water and reheat to create a beautiful dye. Different types of tea will produce different colours. Tea dyeing is ideal to do with children as it is completely safe, but be careful with hot liquids, of course!

With exposure to sunlight, tannin rich dyes can intensify in colour, particularly pomegranate skin dyed fabric which I find often darkens. Avocado stones and skins produce a wide spectrum of pinks, ranging from peach to darker, cool-toned pinks. The pink fades slightly with prolongued exposure to light (more than a garment of clothing would experience if it is well looked after) and the warm yellow undertones from the tannins will become more pronounced.

Even though pomegranates and avocados are edible, their skins and stones are not, and due to the high levels of tannins within them, their dyes can be irritating to the skin and lungs. Gloves should be worn when handling tannin rich dyes and the windows should always be open to avoid breathing in the vapours.

equipment & safety

My essential equipment and some brief (but important) notes on safety.

Equipment

Little specialist equipment is actually needed, but the few items that you do use should be reserved for dyeing and never used for cooking again. My essentials are shown opposite, and of course you need a heat source, as well as a washing line or clothes airer.

- aluminium pot
- rubber gloves
- stainless steel/glass bowl
- stirring spoons
- bucket
- sieve
- muslin cloths
- scales

Safety considerations

- Do not use the same pots and utensils for dyeing and cooking.
- Always work with a window open for good airflow.
- Do not eat food whilst dyeing.
- If working in a kitchen, wipe down surfaces thoroughly after dyeing.
- Wear gloves when taking fibres out of dye pots. Even though the dyes are from plants, they can be irritating to the skin, especially tannin rich dyes.
- Keep lids on pots to avoid vapour escaping.
- Avoid inhaling fumes when inspecting a dye pot.
- Be careful when lifting the lid off a steaming pot as you could scald your wrist very easily. Keep a bottle of lavender essential oil handy for immediate relief if you accidently scald yourself.
- Make sure you have correctly identified the plants you are dyeing with to ensure that they are not toxic.
- If storing dye in the fridge, ensure that jars are clearly labelled and out of reach of young children.

washing & mordanting fibres

How to prepare fabric and yarn before dyeing.

Allow plenty of time

This section outlines all the steps for washing and mordanting your fabric or yarn before you begin dyeing. After completing these steps, you need to wait at least a week before dyeing. It's a good idea to keep a stash of ready prepared fibres that you can dye at a moment's notice.

1. Washing your fabric or yarn

First, weigh your dry fabric or yarn and write down the amount.

Washing fabric

Wash your fabric in the washing machine on a 30 or 40°C cycle (depending on the care instructions that came with your fabric or clothing) with a natural laundry liquid, and do an extra rinse cycle at the end to make sure that all the soap has been rinsed out. Alternatively hand wash your fabric, rinse well and gently squeeze out the water. Then move onto treating your fabric with soya milk.

Years ago, I used to clean fabric by 'scouring' it in boiling water with soda ash but I feel that it was much too harsh on fabric and I still get excellent results by simply washing. Many people choose to scour fabric, and you may decide to, but from my experience it is not essential.

Washing yarn

To avoid getting a tangled mess of yarn, it's best to wind it into a circle right at the beginning. If the yarn came in a skein, you can simply untwist the skein and open it up. If it came in a ball, wrap the yarn around the back of a chair to wind it into a circle. Then tie some string in a few places around the circle. This keeps the yarn together and stops it getting tangled during the washing, mordanting and dyeing processes. Don't tie the string too tight, as you still want the yarn to dye under the string.

Gently wash the circle of yarn in the bath or a bucket of warm water with some natural laundry liquid, then rinse a couple of times. Squeeze out the excess water (by rolling in a towel, if you choose) then move onto the next step.

A circle of yarn

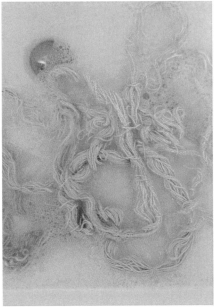

Washing yarn in the bath

2. Pretreating your fibres in soya milk

You can either buy organic unsweetened soya milk from the supermarket or make your own soya milk by using the recipe below. If you're going to buy milk, look for organic, unsweetened milk, with as few additional ingredients as possible. Ideally it will contain just soya beans and water. Both supermarket and homemade soya milk work well. Homemade milk will probably be more concentrated (around 10 - 12% soya) than supermarket milk (which is often 6%). For this reason, homemade milk will go further and mordant more fibres.

Making soya milk

To make 1 litre soya milk, you need:

> 125g organic soya beans
> 1 litre water

1. Soak the soya beans in the water overnight, until the beans have swollen.

2. Put the beans and the litre of water in a blender and blend until smooth.

3. Strain the milk through a muslin cloth, and squeeze in your hands. There will be pulp left in the muslin that looks similar to homous.

4. Add the bits back into the blender with some fresh water and blend again.

5. Strain through a muslin cloth and pour the second lot of milk in with the first.

Applying soya milk to fabric and yarn

1. To mordant approximately 400g of fibres, pour 1 litre of (supermarket) soya milk into a bucket then add in approximately 5 litres of water to dilute the milk. Homemade milk can be diluted even more. Put the damp fabric into the bucket and give it a mix to see how much space it has to move around. If necessary, add in more water to make sure the fabric is fully submerged under the milk. These amounts are just guidelines; the most important thing is that the fibres receive an even coating of diluted milk.

2. Leave the fabric or yarn to soak in the milk for about 12 hours. Try to give the bucket a stir at least once during this period.

3. Remove the fabric from the bucket, squeeze out the excess milk and put it on a spin cycle in the washing machine and hang to dry. For yarn, gently squeeze out the excess milk and hang to dry. It's important to remove the excess milk so there is a very light and even coating on the fibres.

4. Store the bucket of milk somewhere cool. The milk may have separated by the time you get to the next step, so give it a quick mix.

5. Once your fabric or yarn is dry, dip it into the bucket of milk, but only briefly, just so the fibres receive an even coating of milk all over, without rinsing off the first layer. Then spin fabric in the washing machine and leave yarn to drip dry.

6. Repeat step 5 to coat your fabric or yarn in a third layer or milk.

7. Wait at least a week before dyeing your fabric or yarn (longer is even better). This time is needed for the soybean protein to bond to the fibres.

Some tips

- Complete the entire process as quickly as possible before the milk begins to ferment because it will get smelly. The quicker you can dry your fabric or yarn the better, so you can move swiftly onto the next step. If the milk has fermented then it should not be used, so start again with fresh milk.

- In between dips, store the bucket of milk in a cool place. I like to keep mine outside in the shade and cover the top with a piece of wood.

- Spin or squeeze out as much milk as possible before hanging fabric or yarn to dry. Make sure that milk doesn't drip down the length, otherwise the milk will dry unevenly and it will eventually dye with darker patches.

- Put your washing machine on a rinse cycle after spinning out the milk, as the residue of milk can become smelly.

SECTION 6
making a dye bath

How to extract the most colour from your plants
and exploit the mordanting potential of your metal dye pot.

Using a two-step process

Plant dyeing can be as simple as throwing plants and fibres into a pot and heating for a period of time. This all-in-one method can work well for quick experiments, but to produce even colours on fabric or yarn, it is preferable to use a two-step process.

In this section we will extract dye from our dyestuff, strain out the plants to leave a clear dye and charge up the dye with 'mordanting power' from the aluminium pot.

Preparing your plants

As a general guide, I suggest using at least the same weight of plants as weight of fibres (e.g. for 100g fabric, use 100g plants) but you may choose to use more for a stronger colour, or less for a paler shade. There is no right or wrong amount to use; you can just experiment. Some plants may be more potent, such as pomegranate skins which means you can use half the weight of fibres (for 100g fabric, use 50g pomegranate skins). I must confess that in practice I rarely weigh my dyestuffs or fibres; I simply estimate and experiment with what I have available. For future reference, you may decide to keep notes of the quantities you have used alongside small samples of dyed fabric or yarn.

Depending on which dyestuffs you use, you may choose to break them into smaller pieces to increase the surface area.

Making dye from avocado stones

Making dye from mahonia berries

Extracting dye

1. Place your dyestuff in your aluminium pot and cover with just enough water so that everything is submerged.

2. Heat your pot on the stove with the lid on. As a general guide, I would recommend heating your plants for one hour, with a low heat, with the aim of coaxing out the colour rather than cooking the plants. Top up the water level as the liquid evaporates. Each dyestuff requires different levels of heat and for different durations to achieve the purest colour. With some plants, you may like to compare continual heat versus soaking in hot water to see which method works best. (See the following page for some suggestions.) I tend to use a really low heat to begin with (below simmering point) to see how much colour is extracted. Then I might increase the heat to see if I can extract some more colour. It's all a matter of experimentation.

3. After heating your plants, leave them in the pot until the liquid has cooled.

4. Strain through a sieve lined with a muslin cloth. This is important as little bits of leaves or other plant matter can get trapped in fabric or yarn and be tricky to remove and leave dark patches of colour.

5. If you would like to try and extract more colour from your plants, heat the dyestuff in a second lot of fresh water, then combine the two lots of dye at the end.

6. Pour the dye back into the aluminium pot and heat for an hour. This is to get the mordanting benefit from the aluminium. The longer the liquid is left in the aluminium pot, the stronger the mordanting power. I like to leave the dye in the pot for at least 24 hours before dyeing.

Suggestions for different dyestuffs

- Flowers such as dandelions and daffodils need the lowest heat; if you are not careful, flowers can turn to brown mush. Gentle heat helps to produce the clearest, brightest colours. Hibiscus flowers can tolerate higher temperatures.

- Lavender and rosemary leaves first make yellow-green dyes which darken to a brown or grey when left to soak in an aluminium pot. These strong scented plants produce rich, deep colours.

- When dyeing with tea, it's convenient to use tea bags. You can put old tea bags in your dye pot of boiling water and heat until you have extracted the desired colour. Then simply remove the bags to leave a pot of dye.

- Leaves can be steeped in boiling water and left to soak for a few days to extract the dye. Or you can boil them to extract the colour more quickly.

- Eucalyptus leaves need to be heated for quite a long time and at higher temperatures to extract the rich, coral shades.

- Berries can be heated and mashed to extract the most colour.

- Tannin rich dyestuff such as alder cones and catkins produce deep brown shades with little dyestuff; simply soaking in hot water may extract enough colour.

- Bark needs to be soaked in water for a few days (or even weeks) before it will give up its colour in the dye pot.

Avocado dye

The dyes from avocado skins and stones are my favourite of all dyes. Not only are avocados highly nutritious, but the beautiful dyes extracted from the skins and stones contain tannins, which makes them ideal for dyeing cellulose fibres. There are countless varieties of avocado and I find that the rough, dark skins of Hass avocados produce the best pinks. Look out for avocados that develop a pink tinge when they ripen.

Storing avocado stones and skins

The stones dry out well, so wash off any green flesh and leave on a plate to dry out and store somewhere dry. The skins can also be dried but take longer to clean. It's important to wash off as much of the flesh as possible otherwise the skins are likely to grow mould. Lay the clean skins on a piece of cloth and allow to dry in the sun. When fully dry, store in a box or paper bag.

Colours

The skins and stones produce colours ranging from peach to dark pink. Oxidation plays a role in the development of the colour and I find that colour develops further after heating. The first dye bath from stones is usually peach/coral, and subsequent use of the dye baths produces darker pinks. In general, the skins produce more subdued dusty pinks. The colours vary according to the type of avocado, the season and where the fruit was grown. The water type used to make the dye bath also has an effect on colours. Pinker tones can be encouraged by shifting the pH towards alkali at the end of the dyeing process (page 76 for more information). As with all dyes, dissolved minerals in the water also affect the colour outcome.

Extracting dye from avocado skins

1. Weigh your fabric or yarn and use at least the same weight in avocado skins as fabric (e.g. for 100g fabric, use 100g avocado skins). You may find you can use far less than this, depending on the type of avocado, so experiment and see.

2. Add the skins into an aluminium dye pot and cover with just enough water so they are submerged (A).

3. Simmer on the stove for about an hour and a half, with the lid on the pan, stirring every so often. Then leave to cool (B).

4. The skins will have softened considerably. Wearing gloves, squeeze the mushy skins in your hands to break them up into smaller pieces (C).

5. Then heat for another hour to extract even more colour. Leave to cool.

6. Strain through a sieve lined with a muslin cloth. Wearing gloves, squeeze the mush in the cloth to extract as much liquid and colour as possible. (D).

7. You can either discard the skins (E) or try to extract more dye from them by repeating the steps above.

8. You will be left with a small amount of concentrated dye (F). The volume of dye can be increased later according to your needs. Pour the dye back into the aluminium pot and heat for an hour. Make sure that the liquid does not evaporate and add extra water if necessary. Heating the dye now is to get the mordanting benefit from the aluminium. I like to leave the dye in the pot for at least 24 hours before dyeing. A light coloured dye bath will oxidise and usually produce darker shades of pink than originally expected.

Avocado stone dye—
– oxidation
/ peach + pink hues.

1st dye bath

Soybean
jersey

Bamboo
viscose

2nd dye bath

Soybean
jersey

Bamboo
viscose

Extracting dye from avocado stones

I find the dye from avocado stones to be much more potent than the dye from the skins. I have made very concentrated dye baths with as little as 6 stones. Oxidation plays a big role in the way that the colour develops. This is also the case with avocado skins, but is much more apparent with the stones.

An avocado stone has a papery outer layer that can be peeled away to reveal a pale coloured stone inside. If you slice a stone in half, the inside begins to oxidise and you can watch the stone slowly turn darker over a few days; first it turns orange, then parts of it end up almost black. The same happens with a dye bath made from avocado stones; the longer it is heated and left to sit, the darker it will become.

To prepare a dye bath with avocado stones, use the same steps as for skins. I find that the stones make stronger dye, so I often use a 2:1 ratio of fabric to dyestuff, e.g. 100g fibres and 50g avocado stones. Put the whole stones in the dye bath (leaving the papery outer layer on is fine) and as they soften they will naturally split in half, and you can mash them up further to increase the surface area. As they are heated, they will gradually turn orange and this colour will transfer into the water. You can reuse the stones (or the mush that you are left with at the end) a number of times and still extract colour. The second extraction from the stone 'mush' often produces a darker dye bath as the stones have already oxidised.

When using the dye bath for the first time, the resulting colour on fabric or yarn will often be a soft peach. Surprisingly, the next time the dye bath is used, the colour is even darker. If given adequate time for the colour to develop, a few stones can go a long way, making it an economical dye.

dyeing fabric & yarn

*How to dye fabric and yarn to achieve the most even
and colour fast results.*

Slow is always best

Working slowly gives the best results and produces colours that will last the longest. This usually means leaving fabric or yarn in the dye pot for a minimum of 24 hours. The longer the fibres are in the dye pot, the longer the dye particles have to meet and bond with the fibres, thereby creating the longest lasting colours.

Sometimes, however, we may not want to dye for as long as this. When using certain dyeing techniques, such as scrunch or dip dyeing, we may choose to take the fibres out of the dye pot earlier. In this case, I like to make sure that my dye is well 'charged' with mordanting power from the aluminium pot before I begin dyeing. With tannin rich dyes, dyeing for shorter periods of time is often fine, but for other dyes this can mean that your colours don't last as long or are pale.

To dye a lighter colour, it's usually best to make a weak dye bath and dye for a long period of time, rather than taking the fibres out of the pot early. This is to give the dye particles and fibres the best opportunity to bond fully so the colour lasts well.

Yarn soaking in lavender dye

Deciding on your design or pattern

To dye your fabric or yarn an even colour, place the wet fibres directly in the dye pot. Don't try to put too much fabric or yarn in the dye pot at once as it needs plenty of space to move freely to dye evenly. For yarn, leave it tied up in its loose circle so it doesn't get tangled.

If you would like to dye fabric in a particular pattern, perhaps using tie dye or shibori techniques, then prepare your fabric now. To dip dye yarn, you can tie part of the circle of yarn to the pot handle so that only some of it is in the dye bath, as shown in the photo on the previous page.

Dyeing

1. Dampen your fabric or yarn and put it into the dye pot.

2. Depending on how much fabric or yarn you have, you may need to add some extra water into your dye pot so that your fibres are submerged. By adding extra water, the dye will appear lighter in colour, but there's still the same number of dye particles in the dye pot. It might just take slightly longer for all the particles to meet and bond with the fibres. If you would like to dye your fabric or yarn evenly then it's especially important to add in extra water, so your fibres can move freely in the dye bath and receive dye evenly all over.

3. Slowly heat your dye pot and stir every so often to make sure that the fibres are moving freely. Heat very gently for at least an hour and then leave to cool.

4. You may choose to heat again to get a deeper colour. The longer the fibres stay in the dye pot, the more opportunity they have to meet and bond with the dye particles. Also, you will get most benefit from the pot as a mordant and your colours should last longer.

5. Once you have decided to take the fibres out of your dye pot, gently squeeze out the excess dye and leave to dry over a bath or outside in the shade.

6. Store the dry fabric or yarn in a cupboard for a minimum of one week before rinsing. The longer you wait before rinsing, the better the colour will last.

7. Rinse the fabric or yarn in lukewarm water to remove the excess dye. Then wash with a gentle washing liquid. Leave to dry naturally (always in the shade).

How pH affects colour

Some dyes are sensitive to changes in pH levels and produce different colours depending on whether the dye bath is acidic or alkaline. It's simple to test the acidity of dye using pH strips.

- An **acid** has a pH of less than 7. Adding lemon juice or vinegar will make a dye bath acidic.

- An **alkali** has a pH of more than 7. Adding bicarbonate of soda will make a dye bath alkaline. Wood ash is another alkali.

How to alter the pH in a dye bath

Changing the pH of the dye is best done at the end of the dyeing process, by adding either an acid or alkali into the dye bath and allowing the fabric or yarn to remain in there until a colour change has occurred.

The grey fabric swatches in the photo opposite were simply rinsed in tap water which changed the colours from pink/purple to grey/blue. The hibiscus flowers and mahonia berries are naturally acidic (orange pH strip) and the tap water is closer to neutral (green pH strip). After rinsing the excess dye after dyeing, the fabric can then be rinsed in water with a good splash of vinegar to return the colour to purple.

If you encourage a colour by changing the pH, remember that washing the fabric or yarn in water of a different pH may cause the colours to change back again. To maintain a desired colour, you may need to add a dash of vinegar or a spoonful of bicarbonate of soda to the water when you wash your fabric or yarn.

Dried hibiscus flowers

Mahonia berries

Leftover dye

If you feel that the dye bath has not been exhausted (i.e. there are still enough remaining dye particles in the liquid to dye more fabric) then add in more fabric or yarn to the dye pot. It will probably dye a lighter shade, but it is a shame to waste precious dye.

The second dye bath often produces different colours. Many plants contain more than one pigment, so the dye remaining in the pot may be just one of the original colours. For example avocado skin produces pinks in the first dye bath, and then often browner shades of pink thereafter.

To store dye for future use, you can simmer away most of the water to leave a small amount of concentrated dye. Leave this to cool, then pour into an air tight glass jar and store in the fridge for as long as it stays fresh (often several weeks). When you choose to use the dye, just pour it back into your dye pot and add in as much water as necessary to cover the fibres. It must be noted that the colour of dye can be dulled by vigorous boiling and you cannot beat the colours from fresh dye.

Solar dyeing

Solar dyeing is the ultimate slow dyeing method and produces subtly different colours and tones than the standard method of immersion dyeing. Simply place soya milk mordanted fabric or yarn in a glass jar filled with dye and leave on a sunny window sill for a few weeks. The longer the jar is left, the darker the fibres will (hopefully) dye. Check regularly for mould growth and wash thoroughly at the end of the process.

iron water

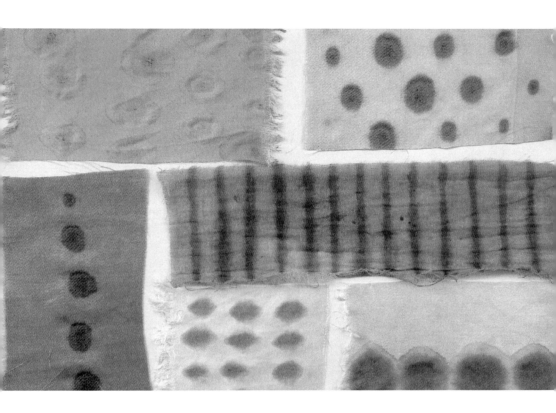

*How to use iron water to easily expand your range of colours
and create simple patterns.*

Why use iron water?

Using iron or rust water is one of the easiest ways to widen your palette of colours. It darkens plant dyed fibres, making the colours more sombre in tone. This section will show you how to make iron water and apply it to your fabric or yarn. Of course iron is not a food grade ingredient like soya milk, so you may choose not to use it. I use it very sparingly but it is useful to have on hand and is especially effective for pattern making.

What is iron water?

Iron water is simply water that contains tiny particles of rust. Rust forms when iron is exposed to oxygen and moisture for a period of time. When rust is applied to plant-dyed fabrics, it has the ability to change the colour of the dye through a simple chemical reaction. It is easy to make iron water by soaking pieces of scrap metal in water to encourage the formation of rust.

After dyed fibres come into contact with iron water, the colour darkens and produces a new colour. Iron water has the advantage of increasing the light and wash fastness of dyes on cellulose fibres, especially when used with tannin rich dyes.

If you choose to dye animal fibres, bear in mind that using too much iron on them can weaken the fibres.

Dye   + Iron water

Alder
cones

Avocado
skin

Pomegranate
skin

Mahonia
berries

Making iron water

1. Take a large glass jar and fill it with water.

2. Add in any pieces of iron that you can find that will fit in the jar. You will probably find that other people are more than happy to donate scrap metal to you. Their junk is your treasure!

3. After a couple of days, you will see that the water has started to turn orange. The longer you leave the jar, the more rust will develop. It might take a month for the iron water to be ready. You can keep a jar of iron water in an air tight jar for a long time.

4. When you begin to use your iron water, remember to top up the water level.

A new jar of iron water on the left, compared to a jar that's more than a year old

Darkening plant dyes with iron water

It is important to never let iron water come into contact with your aluminium pots, utensils or rubber gloves that are used for dyeing. Even after thoroughly cleaning, the iron could still affect any colours that are dyed in the future. I recommend a stainless steel or glass bowl as a designated iron water vessel and reserving a pair of gloves for iron water

1. Gently move your jar of iron water from side to side to mix the rust into the water. Rust is not soluble in water and there will be tiny particles floating.

2. Carefully pour a small amount of iron water into your bowl. Then add extra fresh water to dilute it and increase the volume depending on how much fabric or yarn you would like to dip into the bowl.

3. Wearing gloves, dip your fabric into the bowl of iron water. Depending on how concentrated your iron water is you may need to leave the fibres in the water for a while for the colour to deepen. You will be able to easily see when the colour has changed. (Some people choose to apply heat, but I prefer not to.)

4. Still wearing your gloves, squeeze out the excess liquid and leave to drip dry over a bucket.

5. Pour the bowl of used iron water into the ground and top up the jar with fresh water.

Safety

Always wear rubber gloves as iron water is irritating to the skin and keep away from children and animals.

Painting with iron water

This is an amazing way to easily paint patterns on plant dyed fabric. Depending on the plant dye you use and how concentrated your iron water is, the intensity of the pattern will be different, so you will need to experiment.

1. Lay the dry fabric on a piece of cardboard to protect the table.

2. Gently agitate the contents of the iron water jar by moving it from side to side. Allow large pieces of rust to settle.

3. Dip a paint brush into the water, avoiding any pieces of rust that are floating, and paint directly onto the fabric.

4. When you have finished painting, leave the fabric to dry, then wash the fabric to remove the residue of rust.

A few suggestions

•   Experiment with droplets of water on the end of the brush to form polka dots.

•   Turn droplets of water into brush strokes, to form 'tear drop' shapes.

•   The more concentrated the iron water, the darker the pattern will likely be.

•   Compare the effect of iron water on different dyes. Some dyes that are quite pale react dramatically to iron water.

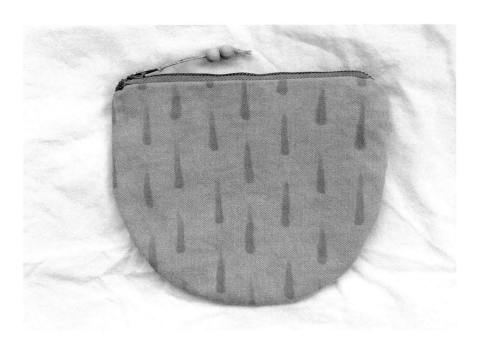

Avocado skin dye and iron water

Avocado skin dye and iron water

How safe is iron water?

I started this book by telling you that I use only natural, non-toxic mordants. Of course iron water is not a food-grade mordant, in the same way that soya milk is; rust is a potentially harmful chemical.

Despite the potential toxicity of iron water, I still feel that it has a valid place in natural dyeing. Rust formation is a natural phenomenon and we are simply making rust through our own chemical reaction. I feel that this is similar to dyeing in an iron pot. The only difference is that iron water enables us to control the application of the iron, rather than darkening the entire piece of fabric, therefore providing endless possibilities for pattern making.

You could argue that dyeing with an aluminium pot is the same as using alum, therefore iron water is the same as using purchased ferrous sulphate (iron in powdered form). But with homemade iron water there is no risk of aspirating fine powders. Furthermore it is not necessary to apply heat to iron water in the same way that alum needs to be heated, so there are no fumes to inhale. Of course, iron water should not be consumed, but neither should any plant dyes that we make.

We can choose to use iron water as sparingly as we like. My favourite application method is painting patterns; very little iron water is needed and the results are striking.

colour fastness

How and why to test the colour fastness of your dyed fibres.

Why colour fastness matters

If we invest time into dyeing fabric or yarn, of course we want the colours to last. This section discusses how the final use of a garment may determine which dyes we choose to use and suggests some methods for testing colour fastness.

Sunlight and repeated washing can cause colours from natural dyes to fade, but we must remember that synthetic colours also fade in the same way. Nevertheless, naturally dyed textiles do need extra care. Ideally, they should be stored in a cupboard out of sunlight when not worn and washed as little as possible. That's not to say that the colours do not last well; I have items of clothing that are still bright after several years of wear.

How will you use your dyed fabric, yarn or clothes?

If other people buy our dyed textiles, then we must ensure that the colours will last well. When I sell my dyed textiles, I only use dyes that contain tannins. I carry out tests on my fabrics so I know that they will last. Also I like to dye clothing for myself first, to observe how colours stand up to everyday use.

If we are dyeing fabric or yarn for ourselves then colour fastness may not be such a concern. It can be exciting to explore the colours of potentially less permanent dyes and we can simply over dye with new plants if the

Dress dyed with mahonia berries

Testing colour fastness

The following tests are useful to carry out when we begin experimenting with a new dye, to see how it stands up to exposure to light and washing. When we assess light fastness, wash fastness and rub fastness together, this tells us how colour fast a dye is. The results of these tests give us vital information that will help inform decisions about the potential end use of our dyed fabric or yarn.

Different dyes have different colour fastness properties so it's helpful to consider what the fabric or yarn will be made into. A cushion cover requires a dye that is particularly light fast as the fabric will remain out in the light. However the dye used for a dress may not need to be quite as light fast as it will only be exposed to light when worn. Of course an item of clothing will need to stand up to regular washing, so wash fastness is particularly important.

Setting up a lightfastness test

1. Light fastness

The purpose of a light fastness test is to see how quickly and to what extent sunlight fades a particular dye. Assessing light fastness involves exposing a portion of fabric or yarn to sunlight whilst keeping the rest of the sample out of the light. After a few weeks the colour of the uncovered and covered portions can be compared to see how much the dye has faded.

One way of doing this is to take a piece of cardboard and cut out a long slot (see photo opposite), then tape the fabric or yarn to the back of the card so that a portion is visible through the slot and the remainder is hidden. Then place the samples somewhere that is bright, but does not receive direct sunlight. I tape my samples to a wall adjacent to a (northern hemisphere) north facing window.

I usually include a control swatch of fabric that I have dyed with conventional mordanting methods, such as madder dyed with aluminium acetate, from my days dyeing with chemical mordants, which is known to have a good degree of light fastness. If another dye that I test alongside the madder fades at a similar rate, then I know that it has similar light fastness properties. If you are beginning your journey with plant dyeing now, then you won't have a control sample like this. In which case, test several dyes alongside each other to see which perform the best.

The results of the light fastness test that was set up opposite showed very little change in colours. After three weeks, the avocado skin dyed fabric yellowed very slightly and the pomegranate skin actually darkened. The other dyes including rooibos tea, red onion skins and eucalyptus showed no change. I tested these samples alongside madder mordanted with aluminium acetate and interestingly that sample faded the most.

2. Wash fastness

When testing wash fastness, we may want to test not only how much a dye fades from washing, but also how much a dye transfers to other dyed fibres. It's important to first rinse the fabric or yarn thoroughly to remove any excess dye, otherwise the results may be misleading.

To test for **fading**, simply take a piece of fabric or yarn and cut it in half. Put one half aside and wash the other half a few times. Then compare the two pieces to see how the colour has faded.

The pink and yellow fabric swatches opposite show very slight colour change from washing, although the small change is more likely due to the pH of the washing liquid. The swatches on the top of each pile are the ones that have been washed a few times; the avocado skin pink fabric looks slightly more pink after washing and the pomegranate skin dye looks slightly greener. In my experience, tannin rich dyes fade very little.

To test for **colour transfer**, sandwich a swatch of fabric between two pieces of undyed fabric and sew around the edges. For yarn, plait a length of dyed yarn with some undyed strands. Wash and dry a few times then undo the stitching or unplait the yarn to see how the colour has transferred onto the undyed fibres. This test is vital if you are planning on incorporating both dyed and undyed fabric or yarn, as dye may transfer onto undyed areas.

3. Rub fastness

It is also worth doing a rub test to see how colour transfers when rubbed against a lighter colour. Simply rub samples of wet and dry fabric on some undyed fabric to check for colour transfer.

A top dyed with avocado skins & scarf dyed with nettles and avocado stones

what next?

Now we have reached the end of the book, I hope you feel you can choose plants with good dye potential and have confidence in producing long-lasting colours on fabric and yarn. Remember that if you use the same plants as me, your colours may look different to the ones in this book. Your shades will be unique to your geographical region, due to the different growing conditions of the plants and your local water. Over time, you can build your own unique palette of colours.

I wish you lots of fun in your natural dyeing adventures!

You are welcome to sign up to the mailing list on my website, **rebeccadesnos.com**, to receive occasional email updates.

To find out more about me or to get in touch, you can:

- visit my website: **rebeccadesnos.com**

- follow my dyeing experiments on instagram: **@rebeccadesnos**

- email me: **info@rebeccadesnos.com**

Thank you so much for buying and reading this book!

glossary

Adjective dye. A dye that needs help from another substance, known as a mordant, to bind the dye to fibre.

Cellulose fibre. A fibre of plant origin such as cotton, linen or hemp. This type of fibre needs assistance from mordants to bind with plant dyes.

Colour fastness. To assess the colour fastness of dyed fabric or yarn, we consider the combined results from light, wash and rub fastness tests.

Dyestuff. A substance used to dye fibres. In this book 'whole dyestuff' refers to plants that are used to dye fabric or yarn.

Fugitive dye. Dyes that eventually fade despite mordanting, e.g. beetroot and tumeric.

Immersion dyeing. The method of dyeing used in this book in which fibres are heated in a pot of dye liquid to transfer colour to cloth or yarn.

Iron water. Water that contains tiny particles of rust. Rust water can be applied to plant dyed fabric or yarn to deepen the colour.

Light fastness. The degree to which dyed fabric or yarn maintains colour through exposure to sunlight.

Mordant. A substance used to fix dye to fibres. In this book the mordants used are soya milk, tannins and iron water.

Protein fibre. Usually fibre from animal origin such as wool, silk and mohair, although soybean fibre is an exception as it is plant derived. Protein fibres readily bond with plant dyes even without mordanting.

Rub fastness. The degree to which colour transfers from dyed fabric to another surface through the action of rubbing.

Substantive dye. A dye that contains tannins which act as a natural mordant and help bond the dye to fibre.

Tannins. Naturally occurring compounds found in seeds, leaves, bark and fruit. They have an important role in plant dyeing and act as natural mordants and fix dyes to fibres.

Vat dye. A sub-category of substantive dyes which include indigo and woad. These require a reduction agent to remove the oxygen to make the dye soluble in water in order for the dye particles to permanently bond with fibres.

Wash fastness. The degree to which dyed fabric or yarn maintains colour through repeated washing.

UK/US vocabulary differences

UK English has been used throughout this book, so US readers may notice a few spelling differences. Below are a handful of words translated for clarity.

avocado stones	-	avocado seeds or pits
bamboo viscose	-	bamboo rayon
beetroot	-	beet
bicarbonate of soda	-	baking soda
soda ash	-	sodium bicarbonate
soya milk	-	soy milk

From left to right: fabric dyed with seaweed, avocado skins & carrot tops

Purple dead nettles

bibliography

DEAN, Jenny. 2007. *Colours from Nature: A Dyer's Handbook.* Published by Jenny Dean.

DEAN, Jenny. 2010. *Wild Colour: How to grow, prepare and use natural dyes.* Octopus Publishing Group.

DOMINIC, Judy. 2011. Bogolan Fini from Mali, Africa/Modified Mud Cloth from Ohio, US. *Turkey Red Journal: A Journal Dedicated to Natural Dyes.* Vol. 17, Issue 1.
Available at:
http://www.turkeyredjournal.com/archives/V17_I1/Dominic.html
[Accessed 21 May 2016].

FLINT, India. 2008. *Eco Colour: Botanical dyes for beautiful textiles.* Murdoch Books.

FLINT, India. 2011. *Second Skin: Choosing and caring for textiles and clothing.* Murdoch Books.

about the author

Rebecca Desnos is a natural dyer who lives in England. Her passion lies in sharing her surprisingly simple methods with others. Well known on Instagram for dyeing with avocado skins, Rebecca shares her daily experiments with thousands of crafters all over the world. Due to much demand, she embarked on a journey to bring her popular eBook 'Botanical Colour at your Fingertips' to paperback.

Rebecca has a varied background in linguistics and interior design, and has been a crafter since her early childhood. Now, as a mother, she finds that plant dyeing is the perfect antidote to busy life. She fills her bag with plants wherever she goes, always in search of new colours. She can usually be found tending to her dye pot in the kitchen.

Made in the USA
San Bernardino, CA
11 May 2017